The Publishers gratefully acknowledge assistance provided by Adrienne Puw, the last living human speaker of Miaow, in compiling this book.

Publishers: Ladybird Books Ltd., Loughborough
Printed in England. If wet, Italy.

'How it works'

THE
CAT

by J.A. HAZELEY, N.S.F.W.
and J.P. MORRIS, O.M.G.

(Authors of 'Cooking Your Dog')

A LADYBIRD BOOK FOR GROWN–UPS

A pet cat can be great fun.

Cats are warm and fluffy, like cuddly toys, and their owners give them lots of time and affection.

And, just like cuddly toys, they do very little in return.

Over thousands of years, we have developed a special relationship with the animals that share our homes.

Dogs have evolved to serve many sorts of human needs.

And humans have evolved to serve many sorts of cat food.

Nasmin knows each of her pet cats has a different personality.

Mushroom is aloof. Cuddles is remote. Pinny is unapproachable. Mittens is unforthcoming. And Professor Snugglepumpkin is stand-offish.

So many characters, but Nasmin loves every one of them equally, to no discernible effect.

Ottolenghi is playing a game with a bird.

The rules of the game are that the first animal to pick the other one up in its teeth and shake it until it is dead wins.

Ottolenghi is disappointed. Wool never gives up like this.

Cats have sensitive tongues and noses so develop strong opinions about their favourite foods.

It is a good idea to buy a lot of your cat's favourite food. That way, you will have something to throw away when she changes her mind.

House cats belong to the same family as lions, cheetahs and leopards.

When the council find out where this family lives, they will almost certainly want to have a word.

This door does not have a cat flap, so it is hard for animals to get into the house.

Dead voles, dead birds, dead rats and front halves of mice all have to stay on the doorstep, along with the cat.

This is the constellation of The Cat.

It can be seen in the night sky, next to the constellation of The Owners Wanting To Lock Up For The Night And Wondering Where Their Cat Has Got To, and just under the constellation of The Shed.

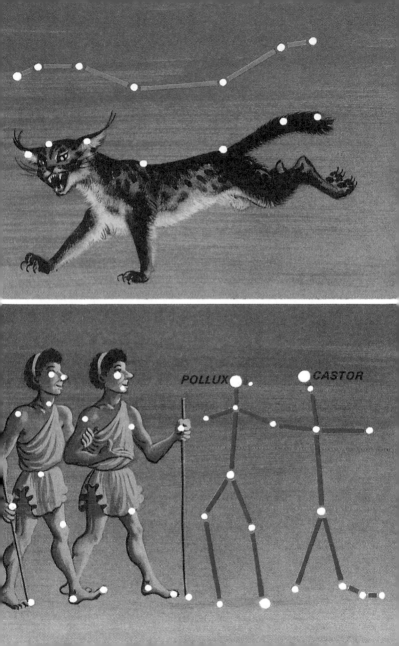

There are two sorts of things in a cat's world — things they are scared of and things they plan to climb inside.

Cats are perfectly equipped for life as predators.

They climb up trees using their sophisticated sense of balance and sharp, forward—facing claws, and climb down using a fully crewed Dennis Rapier XL fire engine.

Bach's cat keeps sitting on his keyboard.

"Go away!" Bach shouts. "I need to finish this important fugue."

He puts the cat on the floor.

Bach and the cat look at each other. They both know what will happen next.

Every morning, Anita puts on a cartoon for Jinkies and her kittens.

The cats do not understand the cartoon but it gives them something to watch instead of Anita on the toilet.

Cats like to hide in boxes.

Imhotep's cat Tibbles–Ra has hidden in this sarcophagus and will not come out.

Imhotep asks his pyramid contractor whether it would be easier to leave Tibbles–Ra in there and convince everyone that cat burials are a thing now.

These kittens are too young to know that cats cannot read like humans.

Instead, a cat waits until its owner has indicated which books and magazines might be interesting by opening them.

Then the cat sits on the book and reads through its bottom.

Cats spend almost three quarters of their time asleep.

This is why they need nine lives to get anything done.

Some cats are working cats.

In this villain's lair, a cat is employed to get blamed every time a secret agent knocks over a pile of metal things while sneaking in.

"It's just the cat," say the guards when the cat strolls out.

Villains' lairs do not really need a cat, but it is a tradition.

Cats enjoy hunting, toying with and dismembering their prey.

Jonathan's cat, Hobnob, has been hunting his Geography homework for forty—five minutes.

Hobnob has found and killed two ox—bow lakes and a relief map of Ottery St Mary.

It is important to constantly take photographs of your cat or people might not know that you have a cat.

If your camera breaks, a simple cat photographing device can be improvised from things you find in a bin, so you need not miss a moment of proving that you have a cat.

They may seem selfish and pampered, but cats can be very useful round the house.

If Zara did not have a cat, she would have had to shred this duvet herself.

Sir Elton John's cat, Paradiddle, has spotted a mouse.

The mouse sees Paradiddle, and pretends to be Sir Elton John playing his piano.

But Paradiddle is not fooled. Sir Elton John is bigger than the mouse, and has not owned a see-through piano since 1975.

The Greek government installed this scratching post to draw out the growing feral cat population.

The laser pointer in the tip means up to 450 cats at a time can be made to chase a red dot around the beach while they are tagged and neutered.

Cressida is playing doll's houses with Marmalade.

Marmalade cannot speak English, hear anything in the normal range of human speech, see things anything closer than six feet, or comprehend events in sequential time.

God only knows what this all looks like to Marmalade.

Sonia has been sent to prison.

She is worried about who will feed Moonwalk while she is not at home.

Moonwalk is not worried. There are six other people on Sonia's street who give him food every day.

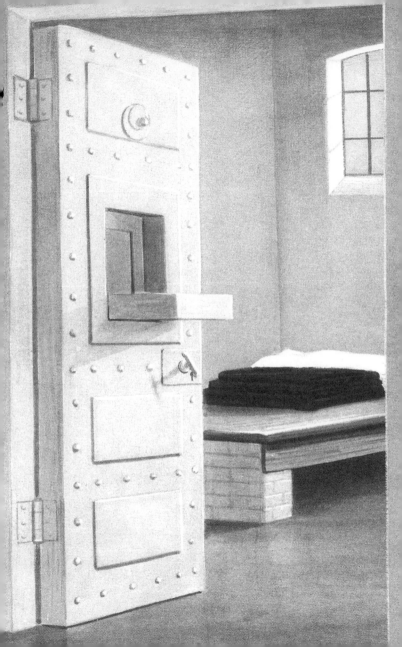

Mimi loved her cat Minimimi very much.

When Minimimi passed on, Mimi took her to a taxidermist.

The taxidermist was surprisingly affordable.

THE AUTHORS would like to record their gratitude and offer their apologies to the many Ladybird artists whose luminous work formed the glorious wallpaper of countless childhoods. Revisiting it for this book as grown-ups has been a privilege.

MICHAEL JOSEPH

UK | USA | Canada | Ireland | Australia
India | New Zealand | South Africa

Michael Joseph is part of the Penguin Random House group of companies whose addresses can be found at global.penguinrandomhouse.com

First published 2016
003

Copyright © Jason Hazeley and Joel Morris, 2016
All images copyright © Ladybird Books Ltd, 2016

The moral right of the authors has been asserted

Printed in Italy by L.E.G.O. S.p.A

A CIP catalogue record for this book is available from the British Library

ISBN: 978–0–718–18433–9

www.greenpenguin.co.uk

MIX
Paper from
responsible sources
FSC® C018179

Penguin Random House is committed to a sustainable future for our business, our readers and our planet. This book is made from Forest Stewardship Council® certified paper.